easyappetizers

easyappetizers

RYLAND
PETERS
& SMALL
LONDON NEW YORK

Designer Luana Gobbo

Commissioning Editor Elsa Petersen-Schepelern

Editor Sharon Ashman

Production Paul Harding

Art Director Gabriella Le Grazie

Publishing Director Alison Starling

First published in the United States in 2004
by Ryland Peters & Small, Inc.
519 Broadway, 5th Floor
New York, NY 10012
www.rylandpeters.com

10 9 8 7 6 5 4 3 2

Library of Congress Cataloging-in-Publication Data

Clark, Maxine.
  Easy appetizers / Maxine Clark.
     p. cm.
  ISBN 978-1-84172-719-6
  1. Appetizers. I. Title.
  TX740.C617 2004
  641.8'12–dc22

                                    2003026837

Printed in China.

Notes

To sterilize preserving jars, wash them in hot, soapy water and
rinse in boiling water. Put in a large saucepan and then cover with
hot water. With the saucepan lid on, bring the water to a boil and
continue boiling for 15 minutes. Turn off the heat, then leave the
jars in the hot water until just before they are to be filled. Invert
the jars onto a clean cloth to dry. Sterilize the lids for 5 minutes,
by boiling, or according to the manufacturer's instructions. Jars
should be filled and sealed while they are still hot. All pickles and
preserves should be processed in a boiling water-bath canner
according to USDA guidelines. For information, see the website
at: http://hgic.clemson.edu/factsheets/HGIC3040.htm

contents

getting started

When entertaining, whether you have planned an informal supper or a magnificent dinner party, you obviously want your meal to get off to a good start. The first course you serve is important because it sets the scene and hints at the delights to follow. Leaf through and you will soon see that *Easy Appetizers*, with its wide selection of delicious soups, salads, dips, meat, fish, and vegetable dishes, has something to suit all tastes and every occasion.

Using only the freshest, spiciest, and most colorful ingredients, the recipes here have a distinctly international flavor, with a range of appetizers from the Mediterranean, the Far East, and the Middle East to choose from, together with some old favorites. What unites them all is that they are surprisingly quick and easy to prepare.

To take the stress out of your evening, many of the dishes can also be made well ahead of time and simply reheated as necessary once your guests have arrived. What's more, you will find that some of them can be adapted to make wonderful light lunches or great picnic, outdoor grill, and party food. So, read on—*Easy Appetizers* is about to open a whole new world of stress-free entertaining.

SOUPS & SALADS

tomato soup

This soup needs to be made with really ripe, flavorful tomatoes—the best you can find. The citrus tang of the lemon will cut through the smoothness of the soup. Add some pesto and basil leaves when serving, for an Italian twist.

To peel the tomatoes, cut a cross in the bottom of each, and dunk into a saucepan of boiling water. Remove after 10 seconds and put in a strainer set over a large pot. Slip off and discard the skins, and cut the tomatoes in half around their "equators." Using a teaspoon, scoop out the seeds into the strainer, then press the pulp and juice through the strainer and put in a blender. Discard the seeds. Chop the tomato halves and add to the blender.

Purée the tomatoes, adding a little of the broth to help the blending—you may have to work in batches. Add the remaining broth, season to taste with salt and pepper, and transfer to the pot. Heat well without boiling. Serve in heated soup plates and top each serving with 1 teaspoon lemon juice, 1 tablespoon pesto, if using, chives or basil, lemon zest, and pepper.

2 lb. very ripe red tomatoes

2 cups chicken broth, or to taste

sea salt and coarsely crushed black pepper

TO SERVE

shredded zest and freshly squeezed juice of 1 unwaxed lemon

¼ cup pesto (optional)

chives or basil leaves, cut up using kitchen scissors

SERVES 4

cream of mushroom soup

A few dried porcini will give a stronger flavor to a soup made with regular cultivated mushrooms. Use large portobellos to give a deeper color as well as flavor.

Put the dried porcini in a bowl, add 1 cup boiling water, and let soak for at least 15 minutes. Heat the oil in a skillet, add the fresh mushrooms, and sauté until browned but still firm. Reserve a few slices for serving.

Add the onion to the skillet and sauté until softened, then add the garlic, nutmeg, and parsley. Rinse any grit out of the porcini and strain their soaking liquid several times through cheesecloth or a tea strainer. Add the liquid and the porcini to the pan. Bring to a boil, then transfer to a food processor. Add 2 ladles of the boiling broth, then pulse until creamy but still chunky.

Heat the butter in a pot until melted, stir in the flour, and cook gently, stirring constantly, until the mixture is very dark brown (take care or it will burn). Add the remaining broth, 1 ladle at a time, stirring well after each addition. Add the mushroom mixture, bring to a boil, then simmer for 20 minutes. Season to taste with salt and pepper. Serve in heated soup bowls topped with a few reserved mushrooms, parsley and a spoonful of crème fraîche or sour cream.

Note If you use a blender to make soup, the purée will be very smooth. If you use a food processor, it will be less smooth, and if you use the pulse button, you can make the mixture quite chunky, which suits mushrooms.

1 oz. dried porcini mushrooms

¼ cup olive oil

6 large portobello mushrooms, wiped, trimmed, and sliced

1 onion, cut in half and thinly sliced

3 garlic cloves, crushed

a pinch of freshly grated nutmeg

leaves from a large bunch of fresh parsley, finely chopped in a food processor

5 cups boiling chicken or vegetable broth

4 tablespoons butter

¼ cup all-purpose flour

sea salt and freshly ground black pepper

TO SERVE

4–6 tablespoons coarsely chopped fresh parsley

4–6 tablespoons crème fraîche or sour cream

SERVES 4–6

An old-fashioned nourishing soup, full of healthy green things. If you do not have sorrel growing in your garden (or available in your supermarket), it can be omitted.

kitchen garden soup

1 fresh bay leaf

1 small cabbage, quartered

4 tablespoons unsalted butter

2 leeks, cut in half lengthwise, and sliced

1 onion, chopped

2 teaspoons salt

8 oz. new potatoes, chopped, about 1¼ cups

a handful of fresh flat-leaf parsley, chopped

8 oz. freshly shelled or frozen peas, about 2 cups

1 romaine lettuce heart, quartered and thinly sliced

a bunch of sorrel, sliced

sea salt and freshly ground black pepper

unsalted butter and/or sour cream, to serve (optional)

SERVES 4–6

Put the bay leaf in a large pot of water and bring to a boil. Add the cabbage quarters and blanch for 3 minutes. Drain the cabbage, pat dry, and slice thinly.

Heat the butter in a large pot. Add the cabbage, leeks, onion, and 2 teaspoons salt, and cook until softened, 5–10 minutes. Add the potatoes, parsley, and 2 quarts water. Add salt and pepper to taste, and simmer gently for 40 minutes.

Stir in the peas, lettuce, and sorrel, and cook for 10 minutes more. Taste for seasoning. Ladle into heated soup bowls, add 1 tablespoon butter and/or sour cream, if using, to each bowl, and serve.

gazpacho

4 Kirby cucumbers, cut in half lengthwise, seeded, peeled, and chopped*

6 tomatoes, peeled and chopped

1 large red onion, chopped

1 red bell pepper, cut in half, seeded, and chopped

1 garlic clove, finely chopped

4 thick slices country bread, crusts removed (optional)

3 tablespoons red wine vinegar

3 teaspoons salt

4 cups ice water

3 tablespoons olive oil

1 tablespoon harissa paste or tomato paste

olive oil, for cooking

TO SERVE

3 thick slices good bread, crusts removed, cut into cubes

1 onion, coarsely chopped

1–2 Kirby cucumbers, cut in half, seeded, and chopped (skin left on), if unavailable, use ½–1 regular cucumber

1 green or red bell pepper, cut in half, seeded, and coarsely chopped

2 hard-cooked eggs, chopped

2 ripe tomatoes, cut in half, seeded, and chopped

SERVES 6

The classic, chilled summer soup of Spain has dozens of variations, depending on its area of origin. The traditional way of serving it is in a large tureen with six separate dishes of garnishes served alongside—these are added by the guests at the table, according to their own taste. Chop each garnish coarsely, rather than finely—the soup should have some texture to it.

Put the peeled cucumbers, tomatoes, onion, pepper, garlic, bread, if using, vinegar, and salt, in a food processor (which gives more texture than a blender). Add the ice water and blend, in batches if necessary, until coarsely chopped, then ladle into a bowl. Mix the olive oil and harissa or tomato paste in a small bowl, then beat it into the soup. Chill until ready to serve, but for at least 3 hours.

Meanwhile, heat some olive oil in a skillet, add the bread cubes, and sauté, turning frequently, until crisp and golden on all sides. Watch them, because they burn easily. Remove from the pan, drain on paper towels, and set aside.

When ready to serve, put each garnish in a separate small bowl, along with a spoon. Serve the soup in the tureen or in soup plates, and let your guests help themselves to whichever garnishes they'd like with their soup.

Note *The cucumbers are peeled and a red pepper, rather than a green one, is used in this version of the soup—red tomatoes and a green pepper and green cucumber skin blended together make a rather unappetizing grayish-brown color. However, to be authentic, use these green elements. If the small Kirby cucumbers are unavailable, use 2 regular cucumbers.

tuscan panzanella

There are as many variations of this Tuscan bread salad as there are cooks—some old recipes don't even include tomatoes. The trick is to let the flavors blend well without the bread disintegrating into a mush. Always use the ripest, reddest, most flavorful tomatoes you can find—Brandywine is a favorite variety, or you could use one of the other full-flavored heirloom varieties, such as Black Russian or Green Zebra, or at least an Italian plum tomato.

Cut the tomatoes in half, spike with slivers of garlic, and transfer to a roasting pan. Roast in a preheated oven at 350°F for about 1 hour, or until wilted and some of the moisture has evaporated.

Meanwhile, put the bread on an oiled, ridged stove-top grill pan and cook until lightly toasted and striped with grill marks on both sides. Tear or cut the toast into pieces and put in a salad bowl. Sprinkle with a little water until damp.

Add the tomatoes, cucumber, onion, parsley, salt, and pepper. Sprinkle with the olive oil, and cider or sherry vinegar, toss well, then set aside for about 1 hour to develop the flavors.

Add the basil leaves and caperberries or capers, and serve sprinkled with a few drops of balsamic vinegar, if using.

6 very ripe tomatoes

2 garlic cloves, sliced into slivers

4 thick slices day-old bread, preferably Italian-style, such as pugliese or ciabatta

about 4 inches cucumber, cut in half lengthwise, seeded, and thinly sliced diagonally

1 red onion, chopped

1 tablespoon chopped fresh flat-leaf parsley

½–¾ cup extra virgin olive oil

2 tablespoons white wine vinegar, cider vinegar, or sherry vinegar

a bunch of fresh basil, leaves torn into pieces

12 caperberries or ¼ cup capers packed in brine, rinsed, and drained

1 teaspoon balsamic vinegar (optional)

sea salt and freshly ground black pepper

SERVES 4

belgian endive salad
with roquefort, celery, and walnuts

4–5 heads of Belgian endive, about 1¼ lb., cut in half lengthwise, cored, and thinly sliced

2 celery stalks, thinly sliced, plus a few leaves, torn

3 oz. Roquefort cheese, crumbled, about ¾ cup

⅓ cup shelled walnuts, chopped, about 2 oz.

a handful of fresh flat-leaf parsley, finely chopped

1 baguette, sliced, to serve

WALNUT VINAIGRETTE

2 tablespoons wine vinegar

1 teaspoon fine sea salt

1 teaspoon Dijon mustard

7 tablespoons safflower oil (see method)

1 tablespoon walnut oil (optional)

freshly ground black pepper

SERVES 4

This salad is a combination of robust flavors and it's a sophisticated way to get your meal started. Developed unintentionally by a gardener at the Brussels botanical gardens in the middle of the nineteenth century, Belgian endive is now cultivated for a good part of the year, and modern varieties have none of the bitterness of their ancestors. When buying, choose very pale endives with only a hint of green; they grow in the dark, so color on the leaves is a sign that they have been exposed to the light and are not as fresh. Also, big is not necessarily better—eight inches is the maximum length for best taste.

To prepare the vinaigrette, put the vinegar in the bowl you plan to serve the salad in. Using a fork or a small whisk, beat in the salt until almost dissolved. You may have to tilt the bowl so the vinegar is deep enough to have something to stir. Mix in the mustard until completely blended. Add the oil, 1 tablespoon at a time, beating well between each addition, until emulsified. If you're using the walnut oil, use 1 less tablespoon of safflower oil. Stir in pepper to taste.

Just before you're ready to serve the salad, add the endive, celery, Roquefort, walnuts, and parsley to the vinaigrette, and toss well. Serve immediately, with a basket of sliced baguette.

tomato salad
with anchovy vinaigrette

1½ lb. vine-ripened tomatoes

1 large shallot, or 1 small
red onion, thinly sliced

coarse sea salt and freshly
ground black pepper

ANCHOVY VINAIGRETTE

1 garlic clove

½ teaspoon Dijon mustard

2 tablespoons white
wine vinegar

6 canned anchovy fillets,
rinsed and drained

8 tablespoons extra virgin
olive oil

a small handful of
fresh basil leaves

TO SERVE

a handful of fresh flat-leaf
parsley, finely chopped

a few fresh basil leaves, torn

SERVES 4

Anchoïade is a Provençal anchovy sauce/dip, which is spread thickly on grilled bread slices, or served with raw vegetables as an appetizer. Here it becomes a dressing for what will hopefully be very ripe, flavorful tomatoes. If these are not available, use boiled baby new potatoes instead, and toss while the potatoes are still warm. Serve this tomato version with a chilled Provençal rosé and lots of crusty bread.

To make the anchovy vinaigrette, put the garlic, mustard, vinegar, and anchovies in a small food processor and blend well. Add the oil, 1 tablespoon at a time, then blend in the basil. Season with pepper and set aside.

Cut the tomatoes into quarters or eighths, depending on their size. Arrange on a plate and sprinkle with the shallot or red onion slices. Season lightly with salt, then spoon the vinaigrette over the top. Sprinkle with the parsley, basil, and freshly ground black pepper, and serve at room temperature.

caesar salad

1 egg, preferably free range and organic

6 smallest leaves of romaine lettuce

½ tablespoon freshly squeezed lemon juice, plus 1 lemon cut into wedges, to serve (optional)

2 tablespoons extra virgin olive oil

3–4 canned anchovy fillets, rinsed and drained

Parmesan cheese, at room temperature, shaved into curls with a vegetable peeler

sea salt and freshly ground black pepper

CROUTONS

1 thick slice crusty white bread or challah bread

2 tablespoons oil and/or butter, for cooking

1 garlic clove, crushed

SERVES 1

This is probably the most famous salad in the world, with the perfect combination of salty, crispy crunch. Note that this recipe serves one person—just multiply the ingredients according to the number of guests you have.

To cook the egg, put it in a small saucepan, cover with water, and bring to a boil. Reduce the heat and simmer for 4–5 minutes. Remove from the heat and cover with cold water to stop it cooking further. Let cool a little, then peel. Cut into quarters just before serving.

To make the croutons, tear the bread into bite-size chunks, brush with oil or butter, and rub with the garlic. Cook on a preheated ridged stove-top grill pan until crisply golden and striped with brown lines.

Put the lettuce in a large bowl and sprinkle with salt and pepper, add the lemon juice, and toss with your hands. Sprinkle with olive oil and toss again.

Put the croutons in a bowl and put the dressed leaves on top. Add the anchovies, egg, and Parmesan, sprinkle with pepper, and serve with lemon wedges, if using.

Note Originally, the salad used a one-minute egg—coddled, rather than boiled—so that the egg became part of the dressing. These days, some people are nervous about uncooked eggs, so this recipe calls for a boiled egg, simmered for 4–5 minutes after the water has come to a boil. The white will be set, but the yolk still soft and creamy.

avocado salad

Avocado is a fabulous salad ingredient—so creamy and delicious, it can really be used as a dressing in itself. You can mix avocado with whatever looks good that day—shrimp, crab, smoked fish, or smoked chicken, all pulled into shreds. Just top it with a few herb leaves if they're handy, grind lots of pepper over it, maybe add a squeeze of lemon juice, and eat it without any dressing.

If using prosciutto, cut the slices into 3–4 pieces. Heat a skillet, brush with 1 tablespoon olive oil, add the prosciutto or bacon, and cook over medium heat, without disturbing, until crisp on one side. Using tongs, turn the slices over and sauté until crisp and papery but not too brown. Remove and drain on paper towels.

Put the dressing ingredients in a salad bowl and beat with a fork or small whisk. When ready to serve, add the leaves to the dressing and turn using your hands. Cut the avocados in half and remove their pits. Using a teaspoon, scoop out balls of avocado into the salad. Toss gently if you like (though this will send the avocado to the bottom of the bowl). Add the crispy prosciutto or bacon, and serve.

Notes To test an avocado for ripeness, don't stick your thumb in it. Instead, cradle it in the palm of your hand and squeeze gently. If it just gives to the pressure, it's perfect.

It's not true that keeping the avocado pit in guacamole or any other avocado dishes will stop them going brown. However, lime or lemon juice, or vinegar will. Add avocado to dishes at the very last minute so it has no chance to discolor.

6 very thin slices prosciutto or bacon

8 oz. salad greens—a mixture of soft, crisp, and peppery, about 8 cups

1–2 ripe Hass avocados

1 tablespoon olive oil, for sautéing

DRESSING

⅓ cup extra virgin olive oil

1 tablespoon cider vinegar or rice vinegar

1 garlic clove, crushed

1 teaspoon Dijon mustard

sea salt and freshly ground black pepper

SERVES 4

DIPS & BREADS

A wonderful combination of fresh spring flavors and colors. Puréeing the peas gives a sweet, earthy base on which to sprinkle the combination of salty, nutty Romano (Parmesan would work very well here, too), and pears tossed in a few drops of balsamic vinegar for sharpness. A delicious start to a light dinner party.

pear, romano, and pea crostini

1 thin French baguette, sliced into thin rounds

2 cups shelled fresh or frozen peas, about 8 oz.

freshly grated nutmeg

1 small ripe pear

a drop balsamic or sherry vinegar

1 cup fresh young Romano or Parmesan cheese, diced

extra virgin olive oil, for brushing and moistening

sea salt and freshly ground black pepper

SERVES 6

To make the crostini, brush both sides of each slice of bread with olive oil, and spread out on a baking sheet. Bake in a preheated oven at 375°F for about 10 minutes, until crisp and golden.

Meanwhile, blanch the peas in boiling water for 3 minutes if they are fresh, or 2 minutes if they are frozen. Drain them, refresh in cold water, and drain again. Put the peas in a food processor or blender, and blend to a purée, moistening with a little olive oil. Season to taste with salt, pepper, and freshly grated nutmeg.

Core and finely chop the pear. Mix with a drop of balsamic or sherry vinegar, then add the cheese, and mix well.

Spread the crostini with a mound of pea purée and top with a spoonful of the pear and cheese mixture. Serve immediately.

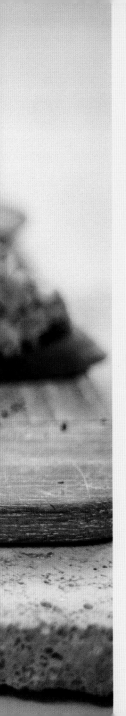

charbroiled eggplant dip

1 large eggplant

2 tablespoons extra virgin olive oil

1 teaspoon ground cumin

1 cup plain yogurt

2 scallions, finely chopped

1 tablespoon freshly squeezed lemon juice

sea salt and freshly ground black pepper

toasted pita bread, to serve

SERVES 6

Cut the eggplant lengthwise into thin slices, about ⅛ inch thick. Put the oil in a small bowl, add the cumin, salt, and pepper, mix well, then brush all over the eggplant.

Cook on a preheated ridged stove-top grill pan or under a hot broiler for 3–4 minutes on each side, until charred and tender. Let cool, then chop finely.

Put the yogurt in a bowl, then stir in the eggplant, scallions, and lemon juice. Taste, and adjust the seasoning with salt and pepper. Serve in bowls or on plates, with toasted pita bread for dipping.

This spicy eggplant dip is like baba ganoush, the Middle Eastern eggplant purée, but it uses yogurt instead of tahini. The eggplant should be charred well to achieve the best smoky flavor.

egg, mascarpone, and asparagus crostini

This is a creamy light topping, packed with the flavor of asparagus. For the best results, don't make this with anything other than fresh asparagus. If you have some truffle oil, you can sprinkle a little over the topping for a special occasion, since the flavors of eggs and truffle go superbly well together.

1 thin French baguette, sliced into thin rounds

1 stick unsalted butter, softened

¼ cup chopped fresh parsley

4 scallions, finely chopped

12 spears fresh green asparagus, stems trimmed

6 large eggs

¼—⅓ cup mascarpone cheese, softened

extra virgin olive oil, for brushing

truffle oil, for sprinkling (optional)

sea salt and freshly ground black pepper

SERVES 6

To make the crostini, brush both sides of each slice of bread with olive oil, and spread out on a baking sheet. Bake in a preheated oven at 375°F for about 10 minutes, until crisp and golden.

Meanwhile, beat the butter with the parsley and scallions, and season with salt and pepper.

Cook the asparagus in boiling salted water for about 6 minutes, until tender. Cut off and set aside the tips, and slice the stems.

Boil the eggs for 6—8 minutes. Plunge into cold water for a couple of minutes, then peel and coarsely mash with a fork. Add the scallion mixture and mascarpone, and stir until creamy. Fold in the sliced asparagus stems, then season with salt and pepper.

Spread the egg mixture thickly onto the crostini, top with the asparagus tips, and sprinkle with a couple drops of truffle oil, if using, or some extra virgin olive oil. Serve immediately.

toasted focaccia
with cranberry beans and greens

Good, toasted bread, with a coarse mash of beans on top and a handful of wild salad greens, is a country treat. If you don't have time to soak and cook the dried cranberry beans from scratch, use canned beans. Dandelion leaves can sometimes be found in good vegetable markets, but if you can't find them, use other greens such as frisée, arugula, or watercress instead.

4 slices focaccia, sliced about ¾ inch thick

2 garlic cloves, crushed

¼ cup extra virgin olive oil

14 oz. canned cranberry beans*

1 teaspoon sea salt flakes

1 teaspoon freshly ground black pepper

2 handfuls of fresh dandelion leaves or other bitter salad greens

freshly squeezed juice of 1 lemon

SERVES 4

Toast the bread on both sides, preferably on a preheated ridged stove-top grill pan or on an outdoor grill. While still hot, rub the toast on one side with a crushed garlic clove, and drizzle with half the oil. Keep hot.

Put the remaining oil in a saucepan and heat gently. Add the remaining garlic and sauté briefly, until aromatic but not brown. Add the drained beans and mash coarsely with a fork. Add the salt and pepper, and cook, stirring, until heated through.

Put the hot toast onto 4 serving plates, spoon the bean mixture on top, then add a tangle of leaves. Sprinkle with lemon juice and serve while the toast is warm, the beans hot, and the salad still bouncy.

To serve as party food, cut small squares of bread to make tiny versions of this dish.

Note *If you are using dried beans, use 1 cup. Soak them overnight in cold water to cover, then drain. Put in a large saucepan, cover with boiling water, and return to a boil. Reduce the heat and simmer until done, 1½–2 hours, depending on the age of the beans.

VEGETARIAN

deep-fried baby artichokes

This delicious dish is very simple and very stylish. It calls for tiny artichoke heads, preferably with violet petals and no more than two inches long. Try it: it is a fascinating recipe, perfect for spring. You could serve the artichoke quarters on individual plates for an elegant dinner party appetizer or, for a more informal gathering of family and friends, let your guests help themselves from a large communal platter which is passed around the table.

10–12 tiny artichokes, preferably with stalks attached

virgin olive oil, for frying

TO SERVE

lemon wedges

sea salt and freshly ground black pepper

SERVES 4–6

Cut the artichokes into quarters lengthwise.

Fill a saucepan with the olive oil to a depth of 2 inches. Heat to about 375°F, or until a small cube of bread turns brown within 40 seconds.

Add the artichokes 6–8 at a time and, using a slotted spoon, push them down hard against the bottom of the pan. Fry until they are crisp and smell caramelized. Carefully remove with tongs or a slotted spoon and drain, stems upward. Keep hot or warm while you cook the remainder.

Remove the stalks and serve the frizzled heads sprinkled with salt and pepper, and with lemon wedges for squeezing.

crudités

Crudités are a classic French appetizer, especially in Parisian cafés and bistros. The selection of vegetables here is fairly representative, but it does vary. Canned corn and tuna are common, as are hard-cooked eggs. You could also try blanched asparagus tips, sliced cherry tomatoes, or wafer-thin red onion slices.

To make the vinaigrette, put the vinegar in a bowl. Using a fork or a small whisk, beat in the salt until almost dissolved. You may have to tilt the bowl so the vinegar is deep enough to have something to stir. Mix in the mustard until completely blended. Add the oil, 1 tablespoon at a time, beating well between each addition, until emulsified. Add pepper to taste. Set aside.

Heat the 2 tablespoons vinegar in a wok. As soon as it boils, remove from the heat, add the red cabbage, and toss well. Salt lightly, and set aside until the cabbage turns an even, deep, fuchsia color.

Meanwhile, put the potatoes in a saucepan with cold water to cover. Bring to a boil, add salt, and cook until tender, about 15 minutes. Drain, peel, and slice thinly.

Bring another saucepan of water to a boil, add salt, then the beans. Cook until just tender, 3–5 minutes. Drain and set aside.

Put the carrots, lemon juice, and a pinch of salt in a bowl, and toss well; set aside. Cut the beets in quarters lengthwise, then slice thinly to get small triangular pieces. Peel the cucumber (if you like), cut it into quarters lengthwise, and slice.

Arrange small mounds of each ingredient on plates, alternating colors. Add a few spoonfuls of vinaigrette to each one, and sprinkle with parsley. Serve with a basket of sliced baguette.

2 tablespoons wine vinegar

¼ red cabbage, thinly sliced

8 oz. baby new potatoes

4 oz. baby green beans, topped and tailed, about 1 cup

3 medium carrots, grated

1 tablespoon freshly squeezed lemon juice

3 cooked beets

1 medium cucumber

a handful of fresh flat-leaf parsley, finely chopped

fine sea salt

1 baguette, sliced, to serve

VINAIGRETTE

3 tablespoons wine vinegar

1 teaspoon fine sea salt

2 teaspoons Dijon mustard

11 tablespoons sunflower oil

freshly ground black pepper

SERVES 4

baby leeks
with herb vinaigrette

Light, lovely leeks in a lively, herb-studded sauce. Serve these at the start of a substantial spread, to allow room for expansion, or as part of a light lunch, with a savory tart, for example. If you can't find sorrel, it will be a shame, but the recipe works without, so don't feel obliged to replace it with anything.

1½ lb. baby leeks, or, if unavailable, the smallest, youngest leeks you can find

2 shallots, thinly sliced

a small bunch of chives, cut up using kitchen scissors

VINAIGRETTE

¼ cup wine vinegar

1 teaspoon Dijon mustard

1 teaspoon fine sea salt

1 cup safflower oil

a small handful of fresh flat-leaf parsley

a small handful of watercress

a small handful of fresh tarragon

3 sorrel leaves

freshly ground black pepper

SERVES 4

Put the leeks in the top of a steamer and cook for 7–10 minutes, until tender. Remove, and set aside to drain.

To make the vinaigrette, put the vinegar, mustard, and salt in a small food processor and blend well. Add about a third of the oil and blend for a few seconds. Continue adding the oil, bit by bit, and blending until the vinaigrette is emulsified. Add the parsley, watercress, tarragon, and sorrel, and pulse again to chop. Add pepper to taste.

If the leeks are still too wet, pat dry with paper towels. Arrange them in a serving dish, spoon the vinaigrette over the top, and sprinkle with shallot slices and chives. Serve with any remaining vinaigrette on the side.

pan-grilled eggplant
with pine nuts and garlic

Eggplant is a versatile vegetable, popular all over the world. Look for really fresh ones, which should have a glossy appearance and be firm to the touch. These days, new breeds have little of the traditional bitterness, so need no pre-salting. This is a quick, light and easy appetizer.

Cut the eggplant lengthwise into thin slices just under ½ inch thick, about 12–16 slices in total. Using a fork, score both sides of each slice several times in a crisscross pattern. Brush a little olive oil on both sides of the slices.

Preheat a ridged stove-top grill pan or nonstick skillet until very hot. Drizzle with a few teaspoons of the remaining oil. Cook half the eggplant slices, pressing them down firmly, for about 3 minutes on each side or until tender and firmly griddle-marked. Remove from the pan, roll them up loosely, and keep them warm. Repeat with the remaining slices.

Add the pine nuts to the oiled, hot pan, and toast gently, stirring them around to prevent scorching. Remove from the pan and set aside.

Finally, put the remaining olive oil in a bowl, add the chopped mint, garlic, if using, and salt, and mix to form a dressing.

Serve the eggplant drizzled with dressing, sprinkled with the pine nuts, and dotted with the remaining mint sprigs.

Variation Add sun-dried or semi-dried (sun-blushed) tomatoes and a little of their rosy oil.

2 medium eggplant, about 1½ lb. total

⅓ cup extra virgin olive oil

1 cup pine nuts

a small bunch of fresh mint, half chopped, half in sprigs

4 garlic cloves, crushed (optional)

½–1 tablespoon sea salt

SERVES 4

warm goat cheese soufflés

Served warm, these soufflés are a favorite appetizer for the cook because you don't have to panic about getting them to the table before they sink! Be sure to butter the ramekins very well so that you can get the soufflés out.

Melt the butter in a medium saucepan, add the flour, and cook over low heat for 30 seconds. Remove the pan from the heat and gradually stir in the milk until smooth. Return to the heat and stir constantly until the mixture thickens. Cook for 1 minute.

Remove from the heat and let cool slightly. Beat in the cheese, egg yolks, herbs, salt, and pepper. Put the egg whites in a bowl and beat until soft peaks form. Fold the egg whites into the cheese mixture.

Spoon the mixture into the ramekins and bake in a preheated oven at 400°F for 15–18 minutes, until risen and golden on top. Remove from the oven and let cool for about 15 minutes.

Using a spatula or butter knife, work around the edges of the soufflés and turn them out onto plates. Serve with arugula salad.

2 tablespoons unsalted butter

2 tablespoons all-purpose flour

1 cup milk

4 oz. soft goat cheese, about 1 cup

3 eggs, separated

2 tablespoons chopped fresh mixed herbs, such as basil, chives, mint, and tarragon

sea salt and freshly ground black pepper

arugula salad, to serve

6 ramekins, 1 cup each, well buttered

SERVES 6

FISH & SEAFOOD

salmon rillettes

Rillettes is a traditional French dish that usually features shredded pork or duck, but salmon and other oily fish offer a delicious substitute. This makes a perfect, hassle-free appetizer, or alternatively, use it as a topping for party canapés.

Put the salmon fillet, skin side up, in a wide saucepan just big enough to fit the fish. Cover with the fish broth. Add the bay leaves, heat to simmering, then poach the fish for 7 minutes. Remove the pan from the heat and let the fish cool in the liquid. Drain the fish and peel off the skin.

Melt 3 tablespoons of the butter in a skillet, add the smoked salmon, and sauté until just opaque. Let cool completely.

Using a fork, shred both salmons together. Put the remaining butter in a bowl and beat with an electric beater or wooden spoon until very soft (butter at room temperature makes this easier). Add the salmons and peppercorns, and beat together. Taste, and season well with salt. Press the mixture into the 6 pots, level the tops with a knife if you like, then refrigerate until firm.

Remove from the refrigerator 15 minutes before serving so the pâté can return to room temperature. Serve with oven-baked toast.

1 lb. salmon fillet, skin on

2½ cups fish broth

3 fresh or dried bay leaves

3½ sticks unsalted butter, at room temperature

12 oz. smoked salmon, unsliced, and cut into chunks

1 tablespoon green peppercorns, crushed

sea salt

oven-baked toast, to serve

6 small pâté pots or ramekins

SERVES 6

Thai fish, shrimp, or crab cakes are quick and easy to make—perfect as an appetizer. If you have time, marinate the shrimp mixture for 30 minutes or so. Keep a few bottles of chile jam in the refrigerator, but you can use a prepared chile sauce if you prefer.

thai shrimp cakes
with chile jam

To make the chile jam, put the tomatoes, chiles, and garlic in a food processor and purée until smooth. Transfer the mixture to a saucepan, add the ginger, soy sauce, sugar, vinegar, and salt, and bring to a boil. Reduce the heat slightly, then simmer fast for 30–35 minutes, stirring occasionally until thick and glossy.

Warm the sterilized jars in a low oven, pour in the thickened jam, and let cool completely. Seal and store in the refrigerator. Use within 1 month.

To make the shrimp cakes, put the shrimp in a food processor and blend to a purée. Add the lime leaves or lime zest, scallions, cilantro, egg, fish sauce, and rice flour or cornstarch, blend briefly, then transfer the mixture to a bowl. Using damp hands, shape the mixture into 24 patties, 2 inches in diameter.

Fill a skillet with oil to a depth of ½ inch, heat for 1 minute over medium heat, then add the cakes, spacing them well apart. Sauté in batches for 2 minutes on each side until golden brown. Remove the cakes with a slotted spoon and drain on crumpled paper towels. Keep them warm in a low oven while you cook the remainder. Serve with chile jam or sweet chile sauce.

1 lb. raw shrimp, shelled and deveined

4 lime leaves, very finely chopped, or grated zest of 1 unwaxed lime

4 scallions, finely chopped

2 tablespoons chopped fresh cilantro

1 egg

1 tablespoon Thai fish sauce

⅓ cup rice flour or cornstarch

peanut or safflower oil, for frying

Chile Jam (below) or sweet chile sauce, to serve

CHILE JAM

1 lb. ripe tomatoes, coarsely chopped

3–4 red chiles, coarsely chopped

2 garlic cloves, chopped

1 teaspoon freshly grated ginger

2 tablespoons light soy sauce

1¼ cups palm sugar or brown sugar

½ cup white wine vinegar

½ teaspoon sea salt

2 preserving jars, about 1 cup each, sterilized (page 4)

SERVES 6 (MAKES 24 CAKES)

drunken clams

Try to find small clams for this recipe—they tend to be sweeter and more tender than the larger varieties. This recipe will serve four as an appetizer, but you can serve it with other Asian dishes, plus rice and noodles, for an impressive banquet.

Tap each clam lightly on the counter and discard any that won't close. Put the clams in a pot, add the broth, rice wine or sherry, garlic, ginger, scallions, and chile. Grind Szechuan pepper over the top and bring to a boil. Cover with a lid and let steam for 3–4 minutes until most of the clam shells have opened.

Discard any unopened clams and transfer the rest to warmed bowls. Pour the broth through a fine strainer, then pour the strained broth over the clams, and serve.

4 lb. fresh clams, well scrubbed

⅔ cup fish or vegetable broth

½ cup Shaohsing (sweetened Chinese rice wine) or sweet sherry

4 garlic cloves, sliced

1 inch fresh ginger root, peeled and sliced

6 scallions, sliced

1 red chile, seeded and sliced

Szechuan pepper or freshly ground black pepper

SERVES 4

fresh vietnamese spring rolls

Vietnamese food is full of flavor. These fresh spring rolls are delicious. They can be made several hours in advance; spray them with a mist of water and cover with plastic wrap to prevent them from drying out. A great hands-on appetizer.

24 small Vietnamese rice paper wrappers (6 inches)*

1 oz. cellophane noodles (1 small bundle), soaked in boiling water for 20 minutes, drained, then cut into 2-inch lengths**

3 carrots, thinly sliced into matchsticks

1 mini cucumber, cut in half lengthwise, seeded, and thinly sliced into matchsticks

6 scallions, cut in half in the middle, then thinly sliced lengthwise

2 baskets enoki mushrooms

fresh mint leaves

fresh cilantro leaves

1 small package fresh bean sprouts, trimmed, rinsed, and dried

2 cups cooked crabmeat, or 2 cups cooked, peeled, chopped shrimp or 2 cups stir-fried ground pork

To make the dipping sauce, put the garlic, chile, and sugar in a spice grinder and blend to a purée. Alternatively, put them in a mortar and pestle and grind to a paste. Add the chopped lime and any collected juice and purée again. Add the fish sauce and about ½ cup water, and stir. Set aside.

To make the spring rolls, first assemble all the ingredients on platters, and fill a wide bowl with hot water. Work on one roll at a time.

Dip 1 rice paper wrapper in the water for about 30 seconds or until softened. Put on a plate (not a board, which will dry out the rice paper). Put a small pinch of each ingredient in a line down the middle of the wrapper, fold over both sides of the wrapper, then roll up like a cigar. (If you find it easier to fold only one side, as shown, let some of the ingredients protrude from the other end.)

Spray with a mist of water and set aside on a plate, covered with a damp cloth, while you prepare the others.

To serve, spray with water again and serve with the dipping sauce.

Notes *The wrappers come in packs of 50 large or 100 small. Wrap leftover wrappers in 2 layers of plastic wrap and seal well.

**If you like, stir 1 tablespoon sesame oil through the noodles after soaking.

NUÓC CHAM DIPPING SAUCE

2 garlic cloves, crushed

1 red chile, seeded and chopped

1 tablespoon sugar

½ lime, quartered and chopped

1½ tablespoons fish sauce

MAKES 24

Bell peppers are ubiquitous ingredients in Italian antipasti recipes. They respond well to broiling and roasting, two methods that develop the natural sugars. Mixed with salty anchovies and sharp pickled caperberries or capers, they really come into their own. This recipe is from southern Italy—easy, elegant, and delicious.

peperoni farciti

4 red or yellow bell peppers, quartered lengthwise and seeded

16 canned anchovy fillets, rinsed and drained

16 caperberries or 2 tablespoons capers, rinsed and drained

a small bunch of fresh marjoram or oregano, chopped

2 tablespoons extra virgin olive oil

freshly ground black pepper

SERVES 4

Arrange the quartered peppers in a large roasting dish or pan.

Using kitchen scissors or a small knife, cut each anchovy fillet in half lengthwise. Put 2 strips into each pepper segment. Add a caperberry or a share of the capers to each segment, and sprinkle with the chopped herbs and olive oil.

Roast, uncovered, toward the top of a preheated oven at 350°F for 20–30 minutes or until wrinkled, aromatic, and beginning to char a little at the edges. Serve hot, warm, or cool, sprinkled with black pepper.

Note Use any color pepper other than green—green tastes too acidic.

MEAT & POULTRY

Yogurt-crusted chicken threaded onto skewers is a delicious way to start a meal. The yogurt tenderizes the chicken and helps the lemon soak into the meat. In summer, cook them on an outdoor grill—the yogurt becomes delicious and slightly crunchy. Otherwise, cook them under a hot broiler.

chicken lemon skewers

Cut the chicken lengthwise into ⅛-inch strips and put in a shallow ceramic dish.

Put all the marinade ingredients in a bowl, stir well, and pour them over the chicken. Turn the chicken to coat it, then cover, and let marinate in the refrigerator overnight.

The next day, thread the chicken onto the soaked bamboo skewers, zig-zagging the meat back and forth as you go.

Cook on a preheated outdoor grill or under a hot broiler for 3–4 minutes on each side, until charred and tender. Let cool slightly before serving.

1 lb. skinless, boneless chicken breasts

MARINADE

1 cup plain yogurt

2 tablespoons extra virgin olive oil

2 garlic cloves, crushed

grated zest and freshly squeezed juice of 1 unwaxed lemon

1–2 teaspoons ground dried chiles

1 tablespoon chopped fresh cilantro

sea salt and freshly ground black pepper

12 bamboo skewers, soaked in cold water for 30 minutes

SERVES 4

chicken liver pâté

This simple, semi-smooth pâté is excellent served as an appetizer, or as a snack or on a picnic. It's incredibly quick to make—it takes less than 10 minutes. It can be eaten warm, but is usually better cooled and chilled (use the freezer for speed). Decorate the butter seal with some peppercorns and extra sprigs of thyme.

Heat a half-stick of the butter in a nonstick skillet. Add the livers and sauté over high heat for 2 minutes, stirring constantly. Standing well back, carefully add the brandy and light it with a match. Let it flame for 1–2 minutes, shaking the skillet, then add the garlic, onion, salt, and nutmeg and cook for a further 2 minutes, until the liquid has almost all evaporated and the livers and onion are golden. (Ideally, the livers should still be pink inside.) Add the thyme and another half-stick of the butter and heat until the butter has melted.

Transfer the mixture to a food processor. Blend, in 4–5 short bursts, to a semi-smooth paste. Spoon into 1 large or 6–8 small china bowls. Smooth the surface with a knife. Melt the remaining butter. Pour it over the pâté, adding a decorative topping of thyme and peppercorns, pushing them into the butter.

Let cool, then put in the freezer for at least 1 hour. Transfer to the refrigerator and chill for 1–2 hours, until very cold and firm. Serve the same day with Melba toast or crisp, toasted slices of baguette, or store longer. Flavors improve for up to 1 week.

1½ sticks butter, cubed

12 oz. chicken livers, trimmed and cut in half

¼ cup brandy

2 garlic cloves, crushed

1 onion, chopped

½ teaspoon kosher salt or sea salt flakes

¼ teaspoon freshly ground nutmeg

2–3 tablespoons fresh thyme leaves

TO SERVE

sprigs of fresh thyme

about 20 peppercorns

Melba toast or slices of baguette, toasted

1 large or 6–8 small deep china bowls

SERVES 6–8

rumaki bacon and chicken liver kabobs

This easy but sophisticated appetizer comes from Hawaii, which has a lively, constantly evolving, multicultural cuisine. Rumaki shows Japanese and Chinese influences, combined with a European touch and typical Polynesian style, exploiting the different cooking styles to excellent effect.

3 tablespoons dark soy sauce

2 tablespoons sake or dry sherry

1 tablespoon brown sugar

2 teaspoons ground ginger

8 oz. chicken livers, trimmed

8 slices bacon, cut in half

about 6 oz. canned water chestnuts, 1 heaped cup, drained and sliced*

8 scallions, trimmed and quartered

16 bamboo skewers or medium satay sticks, soaked in cold water for at least 30 minutes

SERVES 4

Mix the soy sauce, sake or sherry, sugar, and ginger in a large, shallow glass or china dish. Using kitchen scissors, cut the livers into 16 equal pieces, and discard any discolored areas.

Push one end of a piece of bacon onto a soaked skewer or satay stick. Add a piece of liver, 2 water chestnuts, both at once (take care that they don't split), and some scallion pieces set crosswise. Pull the bacon lengthwise, stretching it tightly around the pieces on the skewer or satay stick and securing it back again at the first end so that it neatly encloses the entire rumaki contents in a little package. (Slide the whole little package to one end if it makes it easier.)

Set the completed rumaki in the marinade and turn to coat. Continue until all 16 are made. Marinate for at least 10 minutes, then turn and marinate for another 10 minutes. (Alternatively, marinate for 8 hours in the refrigerator.)

Preheat a broiler or outdoor grill until very hot. If using a broiler, cover the tray with oiled foil. Cook the rumaki 4 inches from the heat for 4–6 minutes on each side or until they are deep, dark brown. Pour the extra marinade over them as they are turned. Serve hot.

Note *If only sliced canned water chestnuts are available, use 3–4 slices per skewer or stick.

vietnamese pork balls
with chile dipping sauce

2 cups ground pork

6 garlic cloves, crushed

2 stalks lemongrass, thinly sliced

1 bunch fresh cilantro, finely chopped

2 red chiles, seeded and diced

1 tablespoon brown sugar

1 tablespoon fish sauce, such as *nam pla*

1 egg, beaten

peanut oil, for frying

sea salt and freshly ground black pepper

CHILE DIPPING SAUCE

½ cup white rice vinegar

2–6 small or 1 large red chile, thinly sliced

1 tablespoon fish sauce

1 scallion, thinly sliced (optional)

½–1 tablespoon brown sugar

SERVES 6 (MAKES ABOUT 12 BALLS)

A delicious traditional recipe that's perfect for an informal start to a meal or a cocktail party. The original recipe is manna from heaven to the dedicated chile-head, but the amount used here is plenty for most tastes. Use fat Fresno chiles for a mild flavor, or tiny bird's eye chiles for blinding heat. Fish sauce is used as a seasoning in Vietnamese cooking—like using salt or soy sauce. If you can't find it, use salt instead (not as interesting, but OK in a pinch.)

To make the chile dipping sauce, mix all the ingredients in a small bowl, stir to dissolve the sugar, then set aside to let the flavors develop.

To make the pork balls, put all the remaining ingredients, except the peanut oil, in a bowl, and mix well.

Dip your hands in water, take 1–2 tablespoons of the mixture, and roll it into a ball. Repeat with the remaining mixture. Put the balls, spaced apart, on a plate as you finish them. Chill for at least 30 minutes.

Fill a wok one-third full of peanut oil and heat to 375°F or until a cube of bread browns in 30 seconds. Add the pork balls, 6 at a time, and deep-fry in batches until golden brown. Remove with a slotted spoon and drain on crumpled paper towels, keeping them warm in the oven until all the balls are done.

Serve with the chile dipping sauce.

bresaola and arugula
with olive oil and parmesan

Bresaola is Italian cured, air-dried beef—flavorful, deep crimson, lean, and succulent. Preferably it should be cut from one piece, sliced very thinly, but it is also available presliced, in packages. This combination of mellow, salty meat with the sharp, savory taste of Parmesan and high-quality extra virgin olive oil is simple, but wonderful. It's a deliciously easy way to get a meal started.

12–16 thin slices of bresaola

a 2 oz. piece Parmesan cheese (it will yield about 1 cup shavings)

a large handful of arugula, torn

4–6 teaspoons high-quality extra virgin olive oil

SERVES 4

Divide the slices of bresaola equally between 4 serving plates.

Using a swivel-bladed vegetable peeler or sharp knife, shave off thin curls of the cheese and drop them on top of the bresaola.

Add the arugula, then drizzle with extra virgin olive oil and serve immediately.

index

credits

Recipes

Maxine Clark Pages 27, 31, 45
Clare Ferguson Pages 32, 35, 40, 53, 56,
59, 63
Elsa Petersen-Schepelern Pages 9, 11, 15,
16, 22, 25, 50, 60
Louise Pickford Pages 28, 43, 46, 49, 55
Laura Washburn Pages 12, 21, 18, 36, 39

Pictures

Key: a=above, b=below, r=right, l=left, c=center

Martin Brigdale 13, 16, 19–20, 31, 37–38
Peter Cassidy Front endpapers, 1, 2–3, 5r,
6l & b, 7, 8–9, 10–12, 14–15, 17, 22–25,
28–29, 32–33, 34–35, 36, 39–42, 45r,
47–48, 52–58, 60, 62
Jean Cazals 9r
Vanessa Davies 18
Gus Filgate Back endpapers, 4–5, 26–27, 30
Jeremy Hopley 50
William Lingwood 44–45, 46, 51, 61
David Munns 6a, 27r, 43, 63
Debi Treloar 21, 35r
Ian Wallace 49
Simon Walton 59

conversion charts

Weights and measures have been
rounded up or down slightly to make
measuring easier.

Volume equivalents:

American	Metric	Imperial
1 teaspoon	5 ml	
1 tablespoon	15 ml	
¼ cup	60 ml	2 fl.oz.
⅓ cup	75 ml	2 ½ fl.oz.
½ cup	125 ml	4 fl.oz.
⅔ cup	150 ml	5 fl.oz. (¼ pint)
¾ cup	175 ml	6 fl.oz.
1 cup	250 ml	8 fl.oz.

Weight equivalents: Measurements:

Imperial	Metric	Inches	Cm
1 oz.	25 g	¼ inch	5 mm
2 oz.	50 g	½ inch	1 cm
3 oz.	75 g	¾ inch	1.5 cm
4 oz.	125 g	1 inch	2.5 cm
5 oz.	150 g	2 inches	5 cm
6 oz.	175 g	3 inches	7 cm
7 oz.	200 g	4 inches	10 cm
8 oz. (½ lb.)	250 g	5 inches	12 cm
9 oz.	275 g	6 inches	15 cm
10 oz.	300 g	7 inches	18 cm
11 oz.	325 g	8 inches	20 cm
12 oz.	375 g	9 inches	23 cm
13 oz.	400 g	10 inches	25 cm
14 oz.	425 g	11 inches	28 cm
15 oz.	475 g	12 inches	30 cm
16 oz. (1 lb.)	500 g		
2 1b.	1 kg		

Oven temperatures:

110°C	(225°F)	Gas ¼
120°C	(250°F)	Gas ½
140°C	(275°F)	Gas 1
150°C	(300°F)	Gas 2
160°C	(325°F)	Gas 3
180°C	(350°F)	Gas 4
190°C	(375°F)	Gas 5
200°C	(400°F)	Gas 6
220°C	(425°F)	Gas 7
230°C	(450°F)	Gas 8
240°C	(475°F)	Gas 9